At Work in the U.S.

Readings and Language for Job Success • Teacher's Resource Guide

Paula M. Jablon • Ellen E. Vacco

Workplace Program, Maynard Adult Learning Center, Maynard, MA

New Readers Press

At Work in the U.S. Teacher's Resource Guide
ISBN 978-1-56420-396-0

Copyright © 2003 New Readers Press
New Readers Press
A Publishing Division of ProLiteracy
1320 Jamesville Avenue, Syracuse, New York 13210
www.newreaderspress.com

Printed in the United States of America
9 8 7 6 5 4

All proceeds from the sale of New Readers Press materials
support literacy programs in the United States and worldwide.

Acquisitions Editor: Paula L. Schlusberg
Content Editor: Judi Lauber
Copy Editor: Marcia Hough
Production Director: Heather Witt
Designer: Kimbrly Koennecke
Illustrations: Carolyn Boehmer, Len Shalansky, James P. Wallace
Production Specialist: Debbie Christiansen
Cover Design: Andrea Woodbury

Contents

Overview **4**
    Key Features of *At Work in the U.S.* 4
    Features of Units 1–4 4
    Features of the Lessons 5
    Using the Lessons 5
    Audio Recording 7
    Unit Tests and Photocopy Masters 7
    Meeting Multiple Learning Styles 7
    Adapting Lessons to Specific Workplace Settings 8

Lesson Notes **9**
    Unit 1 9
    Unit 2 11
    Unit 3 13
    Unit 4 15

Unit Tests **17**
    Unit 1 Test 18
    Unit 2 Test 22
    Unit 3 Test 25
    Unit 4 Test 28

Photocopy Masters (PCMs) **31**

Answer Key for Unit Tests **73**

Answer Key for PCMs **75**

Overview

At Work in the U.S. is designed to help beginning-level ESL students develop an understanding of the U.S. workplace and gain the basic language skills they need to function effectively in it. It is suitable for use in workplace programs, adult ESL or vocational programs, community colleges, and community-based learning centers.

The lessons in At Work in the U.S. are theme-based and include the skills and competencies that students need at work. These themes, exemplified in stories about immigrant workers and developed through vocabulary study and skills-based activities, promote a better awareness and understanding of the U.S. workplace. Although based in specific work situations, the lessons apply to the broad variety of jobs, work sites, and work situations in which ESL learners find themselves. Through practice and reinforcement of needed skills, students will develop the confidence necessary to use English at work and in other aspects of their daily lives.

At Work in the U.S. is designed to meet the varied needs of beginning English language learners. At this level, students have limited proficiency in the language skills they need to function effectively. Some beginners, while able to express themselves orally, have low literacy skills. Others can read and may be able to write to some degree, but have limited skills in listening comprehension and speaking. For students with literacy needs, the text includes exercises for building sight vocabulary and word attack skills, as well as structured writing activities. For students who need to expand their oral skills, the text includes activities such as dialogues, pair work, and class discussions to improve listening comprehension, speaking, and conversation skills, as well as targeted pronunciation exercises. In addition, most exercises calling for written work can be done orally to provide even more speaking practice.

At Work in the U.S. is developmentally structured so that exercises become increasingly more difficult and complex, building on learned skills and vocabulary and gradually requiring greater language proficiency. The lessons are therefore most effectively taught in sequence.

Key Features of At Work in the U.S.

To the Student and Book Opener

At Work in the U.S. begins by providing students (and teachers) with a brief overview of what the text covers. To the Student introduces the main workplace themes and the kinds of skills that students will find as they use the book. This summary can stimulate class discussion of students' needs and goals, as well as some ways in which they think the book can help them.

The illustration and poem on the book opener page introduce the main characters, whose stories exemplify the key themes presented in each lesson. Students have a chance to talk about these people, make predictions, and think about how the characters' experiences are likely to be similar to their own.

Throughout the book, short poems are used periodically to express themes. The use of rhyme and rhythm provides sensory reinforcement to the presentation of language and content.

Script for Listening Activities and Answer Key

At the back of the student text is the script containing prompts for all listening activities. This makes it possible for students to work on or review listening activities in pairs or small groups, prompting each other and checking each other's work. The script is followed by an answer key for short-answer exercises. This allows students to work independently or to check their work in pairs or small groups.

Features of Units 1–4

At Work in the U.S. is divided into four units, with four lessons in each unit. Unit themes are

- Personal Information
- Job Procedures and Benefits
- Job Safety
- The U.S. Workplace

Each unit focuses on the story of one of the main characters, who is identified on the unit opener page. The unit opener introduces the main theme that will be developed in each lesson of the unit. A large illustration, representative of the unit theme, can stimulate discussion that elicits students' prior experience as well as key vocabulary. A list of the lesson titles in each unit allows students to think about the subject matter in lessons to come.

This *Teacher's Resource Guide* provides photocopiable unit tests, which review key points and help students assess what they have learned.

Features of the Lessons

Each lesson focuses on a basic workplace topic related to the central unit theme. The lessons provide

- readings on relevant topics presented through concrete experiences that students are likely to recognize
- exercises that build on the central topic of the lesson, allowing students to practice vocabulary, language skills, and functional skills that relate to the topic
- activities that highlight workplace issues and simulate workplace tasks
- a variety of activity types to accommodate students' different learning styles and experiences

Using the Lessons

This section provides general suggestions for using the main lesson elements and activity types. For specific suggestions for working with each lesson, particularly ideas for extension activities, see the Lesson Notes starting on page 9.

Pre-reading Questions and Illustration

On the lesson opener page, the illustration and the pre-reading questions help students focus on the topic of the lesson. Have students look at the illustration, and ask them what they see. Ask how the illustration relates to the title of the lesson and to their experience. Answer and discuss the questions together as a class.

Words for Work and More Words

These key vocabulary words for each unit are also on the accompanying audio recording. Play the audio or read the words aloud to students. Have

them repeat each word. Listen for correct pronunciation; model and practice if necessary. Discuss meanings. Ask students if they have heard or seen any of the words before and, if so, in what situation. Ask if they know any related words.

Main Story

Each lesson begins with a story about one of the main characters. Each story is recorded on the accompanying audio. Play the audio or read the story aloud as students listen. Repeat all or part as needed. Then ask students some general questions. You can also ask them to summarize the story or give main ideas. Specific details are not important at this point. Have students find and underline vocabulary words from the lists on the lesson opener. They can work alone, with a partner, or in teams. Using the vocabulary words, make up questions about the story and ask the class. Discuss anything in the story that students don't understand.

Reading Comprehension Exercises

Comprehension exercises begin with straightforward yes/no activities and gradually expand in variety and complexity. These exercises focus on skills including reading for information and details, sequencing, getting the main idea, summarizing, drawing conclusions, making inferences, and predicting outcomes.

Students should complete comprehension activities in class. This enables you to observe how they arrive at an answer and to evaluate their progress. Students can work individually, with a partner, or as a group. Strongly encourage them to answer without looking back at the story. Questions are designed so that students should be able to remember the answers. After completion of the exercise, encourage further discussion.

Vocabulary Exercises

Vocabulary exercises should be completed or reviewed in class to make sure students understand meanings. Many exercises incorporate the definitions of words in the items themselves. Others use the word in a sentence, thereby making the meaning clear. For a change of pace, there are periodic word games—word searches and crossword puzzles—to reinforce learning. For these activities, students might find it helpful to work with a partner or in small groups. The puzzles can also be given as homework assignments.

Customize vocabulary work whenever possible. Expand on the vocabulary in the text with words related to students' lives and jobs. Elicit suggestions from the students. You can make a class list or chart of these words, and provide or have students make flash cards. Students can also compile their own dictionaries, adding vocabulary from their workplaces as they proceed through the lessons.

Language Skills

Exercises should be done in class to check understanding and provide needed reinforcement. To add variety and meet the needs of different learning styles, have students put responses on the board. You can reinforce language skills and practice sentence structures by creating scrambled sentence activities. Write each word on an index card or piece of construction paper. Students work in pairs and move cards around to make a sentence.

Oral Exercises

Pronunciation: These activities are found on the audio recording. Play the audio or say the words and sentences and have students repeat or respond to exercise directions. The sentences for practicing target sounds are generally tongue twisters, which make pronunciation practice fun. Some exercises require students to find syllable breaks or identify the number of syllables. Recognizing syllables is a pronunciation as well as a word attack skill. Expand on all pronunciation exercises by using other words from the book and from students' work experiences.

As students respond to pronunciation exercises, listen carefully. You may notice other problems that are not presented in the text but that can be practiced in similar ways.

Dialogues: These activities present one or more models and then ask students to create additional dialogues using prompts in the text or their own ideas. Play the audio or role-play the first dialogue. Students can practice first as a class, then with a partner. Have students create and practice their own dialogues to use at work.

Dialogue exercises can be reinforced by recording students as they respond and roleplay. You can also use the examples in the text as models to create others that more specifically apply to your students and their workplaces.

Listening Practice

These exercises are designed to help students develop their ability to understand oral communications typically heard in the workplace, such as instructions, corrections, or requests. The prompts are on the audio recording. Play the audio or read the exercises. Repeat as many times as necessary to ensure understanding. These activities can also be practiced in pairs or small groups. Encourage general discussion of the prompts. Elicit from students the kinds of oral communications they need to understand for their jobs, and develop additional activities based on those needs.

Reading Practice

In addition to the initial story, each lesson includes reading activities based on other stories, poems, or workplace documents such as forms, memos, reports, and announcements.

The poems in the book are intended to reinforce lesson themes and vocabulary. Play the audio or read the poem aloud. This reading can be used to help students recognize and become familiar with speech patterns including rhythm, stress, and intonation. Discuss meaning and how the poem relates to the general topic of the lesson. Have students repeat the poem after you, line by line. Then have them read the entire poem aloud. Encourage students to practice the poem at home and recite it to the class.

For activities based on forms and similar documents, have students read the material by themselves. Discuss the content and make sure they understand the meaning. If the reading is too difficult for them, read it to them and ask questions to ensure comprehension. Encourage students to bring in forms they need to read.

Writing Practice

Writing is often intimidating for students at this level. The writing activities in *At Work in the U.S.* provide structured opportunities for students to practice typical workplace writing tasks, such as filling in forms and reporting problems. Help students prepare by talking through their responses when appropriate. Give help with spelling if needed. In addition to the activities in the book, use work-related orders, forms, reports, and the like to create additional writing opportunities.

Discussion

Questions and discussion prompts are designed to stimulate critical thinking about issues raised in the lesson. They can be discussed in small groups, with each group then reporting to the whole class. Students can be encouraged to think about why their answers are similar to or different from those of others in the class.

Let's Think about It

These activities should always be done in class for maximum discussion opportunity. Activity topics are relevant to students' work life and can stimulate debate and cultural comparison as well as discussion. Ask students to justify their answers and points of view.

Cultural Exchange

Use these topics to encourage spontaneous discussion as students respond. Don't be overly concerned with grammar and pronunciation. Point out similarities of cultures as well as differences. It is important to create an atmosphere of tolerance and respect in your classroom. These discussions help to break down cultural stereotypes and barriers. If appropriate, students can also write their thoughts in a journal.

Application

These exercises are designed to connect the work in the text to tasks students will actually perform on the job. If any students are at the same workplace, encourage them to work together on application activities.

Audio Recording

The audio recording that accompanies *At Work in the U.S.,* available on cassette or audio CD, provides an oral presentation of selected student book materials to enhance students' listening and speaking skills. The recording models natural pronunciation

and intonation and exposes learners to different voices. It can be used for class or small-group practice or can provide students with independent practice opportunities. The audio recording includes the Words for Work and More Words lists, the stories that introduce each lesson, all poems and stories for Reading Practice activities, word lists in Pronunciation activities, model dialogues and prompts for Dialogue exercises, and prompts for all Listening Practice exercises. Extensive practice understanding natural language and producing comprehensible speech is essential for meeting the extensive listening and speaking demands of any workplace.

Unit Tests and Photocopy Masters

This *Teacher's Resource Guide* contains photocopiable tests, one for each student book unit, to provide a measure of progress for both students and teachers. Each test covers skills and content from the whole unit. Test activities resemble the kinds of exercises used in the student book; since students already have experience with carrying out those activities, test anxiety can be kept to a minimum. A section of photocopy masters with activities to supplement each lesson and unit follows the unit tests. These activities can be used in class or assigned for homework to review and expand on lesson material. Many of them are suitable for customizing to learners' workplaces or interests.

Meeting Multiple Learning Styles

At Work in the U.S. provides a wide variety of activity types throughout the student book and the photocopy masters. Additional types are suggested throughout the Lesson Notes. This variety is essential to meet the varied needs of students with different learning styles. It also serves to reinforce the material more effectively. Beyond what is provided in the student book and this *Teacher's Resource Guide,* you can easily introduce additional modes of presenting and practicing the material. For example, have students do written exercises orally before they write, or have them review the answers orally. Have students listen to directions for an activity instead of reading them. After students read and discuss a story, elicit an oral retelling by using drawings to represent key nouns from the story. Review vocabulary with flash cards. Expand on readings or exercises by having students create their own questions and exchange them with others in the class.

Adapting Lessons to Specific Workplace Settings

At Work in the U.S. develops the basic language skills, thinking skills, and personal qualities, as well as the workplace competencies identified by the Secretary's Commission on Achieving Necessary Skills (SCANS). If students are not yet working, this material can help prepare them for future employment. For students who are working, the activities provide a framework to transfer what they have learned in class to their jobs and to bring materials or issues from work to class.

Using the material in the text as a springboard, connect the classroom to the work sites. Whenever possible, use work-related vocabulary drawn from students' own experience and needs. Compare the forms, signs, rules, and so on that students have at work to those in the text. Relate the stories in the text to students' personal experiences. If some students are not yet working, connect the lessons in the text to other aspects of their lives. For example, giving personal information, following safety signs and labels, and understanding benefits are relevant to everyone.

It is important for students, and for their employers as well, to see that class work is directly relevant to the job. This connection is key to the success of any workplace program or workforce preparation program. It motivates students to learn and helps employers evaluate and justify support of a program. Therefore, as much as possible, connect the classroom to work. Suggested methods include the following:

- Educate yourself about students' jobs; if possible, interview students, supervisors, and other workplace personnel.
- Visit students' work sites to make note of features in the surroundings, environment, equipment, and materials.
- Communicate regularly with supervisory personnel to monitor progress, ongoing needs, work changes, problems, etc.
- Relate the material in the text to students' work conditions and experiences.

Lesson Notes

These Lesson Notes, for selected activities in each lesson, focus in particular on suggestions for reinforcement and extension activities, as well as on ways to vary presentation of specific exercises in order to help students better understand and retain the material in the text.

Book Opener (page 5)

Look at the illustration. Ask students what they see. Read the poem or play it on the audio as students follow along. Then connect the poem to the illustration by asking students to look at the illustration as you read or play the poem a second time. Ask students questions about the poem to check comprehension; have them relate the poem to the people in the illustration. Ask follow-up questions about their own lives and their jobs. Finally, recite the poem together.

Unit 1

Lesson 1: In the U.S.

Students need to be able to communicate basic information about themselves at work and elsewhere. This lesson helps students understand and give personal information.

Story (page 8)
After reading the story, have a class discussion about where students live now. Ask if they live in a city or in a town, in an apartment or in a house, in a big or small home, and so on.

Oral Practice (pages 11 to 12)
Pronunciation: Show students how to pronounce the two sounds of *th*. For expansion, contrast the sounds of *t* and *z* with the sound of *th*. Have students practice with a mirror.

Dialogue: As an additional exercise, have students close their books. Ask the questions again. Students should be able to answer clearly and without hesitation. This dialogue can also be used for evaluation.

Reading Practice (page 13)
Discuss the meaning of the poem with the class. Follow up by creating one or more language experience stories in which students share their own experiences and observations. Write these stories on the board. Read them together. Have students copy from the board, or you can copy and transfer them to a handout.

Application (page 13)
Have students use their stories to introduce themselves to the class. Encourage them to say the information without reading it. As follow-up, you can make name cards or help students make their own. For the first few classes, place these cards in front of each student. This helps everyone get acquainted and remember names.

Bring in a map of the world and hang it up. Ask students to show the class their native countries. Put a star or pin on each student's country. If many students are from the same country, have them show their city, town, or area. This is also an opportunity for students to tell their stories about coming to the U.S.

Lesson 2: At ESL Class

Students need to understand forms and fill them out correctly. The material in this lesson should be reinforced with forms from students' workplaces.

Story (page 15)
After reading the story, ask students if they were nervous when they started ESL class, and why or why not. Ask if they are nervous in class now and, if so, why. If possible, discuss other activities that make them nervous.

Vocabulary (page 16)
Students may not understand the directions *Circle the word that does not belong.* The first time, you may need to do this exercise with the class to model what is required.

Reading Practice (page 20)
Follow up by making this an oral activity. Have students use the information to "introduce" their

partners to the rest of the class. Encourage students to say the information, not read it, if possible.

Cultural Exchange (page 21)

Extension: Ask students how they address people in various positions in their native countries (first name; Mr., Mrs., etc.; other forms of address). Ask if their first or last names are common ones in their countries and if the names have particular meanings. If students are comfortable with the question, ask if they use a different name in the U.S. and, if so, why. Ask also if they know other people who use a different name in the U.S.

Application (page 21)

Writing Practice: For extension, ask each student to say and spell his or her address and the employer's address. Check for clarity of pronunciation.

Lesson 3: Classmates & Co-workers

When students need to communicate with people at work, they often must deal with people from different cultures and backgrounds. This lesson focuses on trying to understand and communicate with co-workers.

Story (page 23)

After reading the story, discuss the makeup of the class. Identify what countries students are from and if any are from the same country. Ask if any work in the same place and, if so, ask if they work in the same department.

Language Skills (page 25)

For extension, go around the class and ask students about the departments in which they work. Ask one student where he or she works. Then ask another student where the first student works. Have students answer in full sentences. For example:

Teacher: Cho, where do you work?

Cho: I work in the housekeeping department.

Teacher: Manny, where does Cho work?

Manny: Cho works in the housekeeping department.

If students are not working, use this round-robin technique to ask them what country they come from, where they live now, or what languages they speak.

Oral Practice (page 26)

Pronunciation: If students have difficulty producing the sound of the letter *h*, have them hold a piece of tissue in front of their mouths and try to pronounce the sound until they can make the tissue move.

Presentation: Copy the organization chart on the board. Have students go to the board one by one, fill in their own information, and tell the class about it. If many students work in the same place or department, this exercise will become repetitive. In that case, vary it by staggering the presentations. Do some one day, some the next, and so on. For review and further practice, record each student.

More Practice: Vocabulary (page 28)

Use this exercise to practice pronunciation of countries and nationalities. Follow up with your own matching exercise, including the countries represented in your classroom. Elicit from students the countries from which their co-workers come and include those countries in the exercise. As a variation, you can make a matching exercise using countries and languages.

Cultural Exchange (page 28)

If possible, have students follow up the discussion by giving a short presentation about their countries. They can include the topics discussed in the directions for the exercise. Help them make a poster showing flags of their native countries and hang it in the classroom.

Have the class host an international day. This could be held to celebrate a U.S. holiday, students' holidays, or the end of the school year. Include food, clothing, music, etc. Decorate the room with pictures or, if possible, crafts and other items representing the students' countries. Students can also make invitations, cards, or a poster with "Welcome," "Happy Holidays," or another appropriate message written in each one's native language.

Application (page 29)

For extension, ask students what topics they talk about with their co-workers. Have them role-play a conversation with a co-worker.

Lesson 4: Maria's Job

This lesson helps students define work-related language goals. Goal setting helps students understand their own needs, monitor learning, and evaluate progress.

Pre-reading Illustration and Questions (page 30)

Discuss and make a list of the jobs students have now or have had in the past. Help with vocabulary if needed. Students may want to create a poster or collage of their own jobs, similar to the illustration.

Language Skills (page 33)

After students answer the questions in exercise B, have them brainstorm other questions. Encourage them to include common work-related words. Then one student asks a classmate a question. That classmate answers and asks another classmate a question (the same or a different one), and so on.

More Practice: Measurement (page 34)

For follow-up, bring in different tools of measurement and practice with them. Students can bring in measuring tools they have at work or at home. Have students demonstrate and practice with them.

Cultural Exchange (page 35)

Extension: Food is a universal and unifying topic. Everyone can participate in the discussion. Prepare for having students bring in foods or recipes with general discussion. Start by asking questions, for example: *Do you like American food? What do you like? What don't you like? Are there foods you haven't tried? Why?* Bring in or have students bring in supermarket ads, menus, or a picture dictionary, and review names of common foods.

Application (page 36)

For follow-up, tally students' responses and make a class chart. Then discuss the responses of the class as a whole.

Unit 2

Lesson 5: A Busy Schedule

Workers need to be able to read work schedules, know how to request a change, and understand acceptable reasons for doing so. This lesson deals with schedules and the American concept of time.

Story (page 39)

After reading the story, have a class discussion about working and child-care issues. Ask students who takes care of their children, if they are in a good situation, if their child care is expensive or reasonable, and so on.

Language Skills (page 41)

Extend exercise B by adding other verbs and prepositional phrases that relate to students' lives and jobs.

Listening Practice (page 42)

Follow up by dictating other numbers, dates, and times. In particular, include numbers ending in *-teen* and *-ty*. Contrast the numbers (*e.g., thirteen, thirty*). Then turn around so students can't see you form the words, and dictate other numbers.

Let's Think about It (page 45)

After reviewing students' responses, discuss other good or bad reasons for being late.

Application (page 45)

Students may not be able to write a dialogue, but may have sufficient verbal skills to role-play a conversation without a script. Or the class could write a dialogue together, memorize it, and have pairs present it.

Encourage students, as they prepare their work schedule, to include details such as carrying out job procedures and tasks, taking breaks, and so on.

Lesson 6: Ana's New Job

Workers not only have to understand job procedures, but they often have to explain to others what they do and where things are at work (*e.g.,* for inspections and ISO qualifications). In this lesson, students practice following directions and locating supplies, as well as describing their jobs.

Story (page 47)

After reading the story, ask your students if they have inspections at work. If so, ask who does the inspection, how often one occurs, what happens, and so on.

Listening Practice (page 51)

Following Directions: After completing the first activity as a model, customize the listening task with directions that your students need on their own jobs.

To help students understand oral instructions in general, play games like Simon Says including directions such as *sit down*, *stand up*, *turn around*, *look to the left*, *look to the right*, etc.

Application (page 53)

If students need additional support in telling about their jobs, write the following words on the board: *Department, Job, First I __, Then I __, Next I __,* and *I use __*. Students can use these words as prompts. For review and further practice, record students' presentations. Then ask students questions about their classmates' jobs. If students aren't working, they could describe their daily routine at home or in class.

For variations, have students bring tools or other objects they use at work and explain how they use them. If possible, go to students' work sites and have them explain their jobs. Using a language experience approach, have the class compose a paragraph about their jobs, for example: *Lucia works in the laundry. She washes the sheets and towels. Minh works in maintenance. . . .*

Lesson 7: Time Off

Workers have to understand when they can appropriately take time off as well as the importance of notifying their employers if they won't be coming to work. This lesson gives students an awareness of these issues and practice in the procedures they need to follow.

Pre-reading Questions (page 54)

In addition to the questions here, ask students how they ask for time off and who they have to call or talk to.

Language Skills (page 57)

Expand on exercise B by having students make up questions using the verb *have,* asking about illnesses and work issues, for example: *Do you have a headache? Do you have the scissors? Do you have a day off?* Students can work as a class or with a partner, preparing questions and then asking and answering them.

Listening Practice (page 59)

After practicing with the recorded message, dictate messages on other issues, including calling in late, reporting an absence, or requesting supplies. If possible, include messages that apply to students' jobs or work sites. Also, have students dictate messages to each other on a variety of topics.

Application (page 61)

After students practice calling in sick with the exercise in the book, have them call their boss, the Human Resources office where they work, or you; have them leave a message on an answering machine. Arrange this ahead of time with the boss or HR personnel so that they understand that the message is only practice.

As students practice asking for time off, encourage class discussion of workplace policies for requesting vacation and other time off. Use item 2 to have students develop role-plays between a boss and an employee.

Lesson 8: Getting Paid

In this lesson students learn about paychecks and related issues. They learn to read their pay stubs and understand what deductions have been taken.

Story (page 63)

After reading the story, have a class discussion about paychecks. Ask students if they understand everything on their pay stubs and what the specific taxes are used for. Ask students if they ever work overtime and, if so, how often. Ask if they like overtime, and why or why not.

Language Skills (page 65)

For extension, show students a picture of people working (something site- or job-specific is best). Ask the class questions requiring answers in the present continuous tense. Students can also work in pairs to write about pictures of people working.

For further extension, go around the class and ask each student *What are you doing? What are you wearing?* Answers should not be duplicated. For more extended practice, make up questions beginning with *who, what, where,* and *why,* using the present continuous tense. (Suggested verbs: *doing, wearing, working, reading, smiling, looking at,* etc.) Write each question on a card. Students pick one or two cards each. The first student calls on a classmate by name and asks a question. The second student answers the question and then calls on a third classmate, who answers and then asks another question, and so on. Continue until everyone has had a chance to ask and to answer.

Reading Practice (page 67)
After reading the poem, have a class discussion about benefits and taxes. Ask questions, for example: *What kind of health insurance do you have? What does it cover? What is Social Security used for?* You could also have the class make a list of other taxes they pay (sales, property, school, town or county, etc.). Ask students if they think taxes are high in the U.S. Have them compare taxes here to those in their native countries.

Unit 3

Lesson 9: Change Is Hard

Working with new people, new products, and new machines can create tensions that affect productivity and even safety. In the context of a changing workplace, this lesson introduces students to key safety vocabulary on signs and labels and teaches them when and how to ask for help.

Story (page 72)
After reading the story, have students reread the third paragraph. As a class, discuss teamwork. Ask if students work in teams, or with one or two other people but not in a team structure. Ask if they like teamwork, and why or why not. Help them discuss what is good about working in teams and what is not so good about it.

Comprehension (page 73)
Point out new directions to students. Explain *There may be one or two answers.* If necessary, do the first item or two as a class to demonstrate.

Language Skills (page 75)
Have students further personalize the exercise by making additional sentences about things they never do, seldom do, usually do, etc., at work and at home.

For extension, contrast the present and present continuous tenses by asking questions, for example: *Do you work every day? Are you working now?* Give students other verbs applicable to work, such as *finish, do, go, read, speak,* or *take.* Have them work together to make sentences using both tenses. This can be done as a competition.

Reading Practice (page 76)
Ask students if they know someone at work who sometimes needs help. Have them explain what they do if someone needs help.

Discussion (page 76)
Extend the discussion by asking students when they need help at work. Make a class list. Using this list, help students create one or more dialogues between a boss and a worker asking for help. Have pairs of students role-play the dialogues. If students are not working, have them make a list and create dialogues based on any time they need to ask for help, and then role-play.

Application (page 77)
Ask students if they use dangerous products at work or at home. Ask what the products are. If possible, have students bring in or copy labels from those products to share with the class.

Ask for permission to walk, with the class, around a workplace where one of your students works. Point out safety signs and labels. If it is permitted, you may want to take pictures of them.

Lesson 10: Safety on the Job

It is essential that workers understand and follow safety rules. They may also have to wear safety gear and use safety equipment. In this lesson students learn about safety at work.

Story (page 79)

After reading the story, ask students who told them about safety at work. Find out if they have safety training, teams, or some similar structure where they work.

Language Skills (page 82)

For follow-up, give students verbs that they might use at work, such as *wait, wash, finish,* or *fix.* Have them make sentences in the past tense. Do this as a class activity, in pairs, or for homework.

Listening Practice (page 83)

Have students repeat each word. Make sure they pronounce the endings distinctly. For extension, add other verbs that students know. To further help students remember the distinction in past-tense endings, make lists of verbs with contrasting endings.

Application (page 85)

As a class activity, make a list of all the safety rules students bring to class. Post this list, and periodically check students' comprehension.

Lesson 11: Accidents Can Happen

Accidents are common at many workplaces. In this lesson students learn about preventing accidents and following procedures when there is an accident.

Vocabulary (page 89)

Exercise B may be difficult or unfamiliar for students. If so, do it together as a class.

Language Skills (page 90)

For more practice, make flash cards of irregular verbs. Put the present tense of the verb on one side and the past tense on the other. Have students practice seeing one form and giving the other form. Students can then use these cards individually or in pairs.

For variation, make two sets of cards with present and past tenses of the same verbs. Shuffle and place all cards facedown in rows. Students take turns finding present-/past-tense matches. When a match is made, the student who made it must use the past-tense verb in a sentence. Then he or she keeps the two cards. The student with the most cards wins.

Application (page 92)

For item 1, bring a first-aid kit to class and help students identify the items and what they are used for. In item 2, if there is no accident form available, use the one in the book as an example and create your own.

Lesson 12: Reporting a Problem

Workers need to know how and when to report problems. They need to know that this is everyone's responsibility and important for safety, efficiency, and quality of work. This lesson gives students the tools they need to identify and report workplace problems.

Story (page 94)

After reading the story, ask students what kind of problems they have at work. Encourage them to discuss a variety of problems, for example, with equipment, supplies, or people.

Language Skills (page 97)

Extend by giving students other verbs that they might use at work, such as *get, have, tell,* or *bring.* Have them use the verbs to make sentences in the past tense.

For more practice, separate the class into teams. Put a list of present-tense irregular verbs on the board. Each team comes up with the corresponding past tense of all the verbs. One person records the past-tense forms. As a variation, put two identical lists on the board. Members of each team take turns going to their list of verbs and writing the past tense of one verb until the list is complete. The first team to get all the correct answers wins.

Application (page 99)

Review the pronunciation of information needed in an emergency, especially name and address. Have students practice spelling the information as well. If possible, record this exercise for further practice and review.

Unit 4

Lesson 13: Laid Off

Layoffs are stressful for everyone. Workers often need information when dealing with a layoff. In this lesson students learn about where to go and what to do to find a new job.

Pre-reading Illustration and Questions (page 101)

Discuss the illustration with the class. Ask students questions about the ads. Ask them where they see bulletin boards and what they find on them. Then have them answer and discuss the pre-reading questions.

Story (page 102)

Ask students if they know anyone who has been laid off and if layoffs worry them. After reading the story, ask students if they were ever laid off and, if so, what they did to manage until they found a new job and how they found another job.

Reading Practice (page 106)

Read the ads with the students. Make sure they understand the ads, particularly the abbreviations, before answering the questions. For extension, bring in the Help Wanted section of the local newspaper. Have students read some of the ads. Review vocabulary and abbreviations. Make a list of new words.

Lesson 14: At the Store

There are many things to learn when beginning a new job. In this lesson students learn about adjusting to a new place, finding their way around by asking for and getting directions, and understanding unions.

Story (page 111)

After reading the story, ask students if they had a lot to learn when they first started their jobs. Encourage them to tell who helped them and how they felt. Ask if it was hard or easy to learn about the new job.

Language Skills (page 114)

Extend by adding other words of direction, such as *near, around the corner from, turn left, turn right,*

etc. Using other floor plans, your classroom, the picture of the storage closet on page 50, etc., give students the locations of objects, for example, *I see something in the back of the room, next to __, behind __.* Students guess the object. Alternatively, using the places or pictures suggested above, ask students to find specific locations or objects *(Where is __?)* and identify them using words of direction and location.

Lesson 15: Getting Along with Sam

There are often personality clashes at work. Trying to understand and get along with people in a new culture can be particularly frustrating. This lesson focuses on dealing with difficult co-workers.

Pre-reading Illustration (page 117)

Ask students what they think is happening in the illustration. Help them to speculate on why the person is standing to one side and to discuss how they think he feels.

Story (page 118)

After reading the story, ask students if they ever had a problem like this. Ask how they felt and what they did about the problem.

Comprehension (page 119)

In exercise B, the ending can be written as prose or as a dialogue. Alternatively, if it suits their skills better, students can role-play an ending rather than write it.

More Practice: Language Skills (page 124)

Have students take turns asking and answering these questions. For extension, have them brainstorm additional questions with *when* and *where.* Write the questions on the board or give students a written list, and have them practice with one another.

Application (page 124)

Use this exercise to generate a class vocabulary list of things students use and encounter or deal with in their jobs.

Lesson 16: Understanding the U.S.

Most people living and working in a new culture want and need to understand what the expectations are. This lesson focuses on standards of social behavior and job performance in the U.S.

Story (page 126)

After reading the story, discuss the concept of performance evaluations or reviews and why they are done. Ask students if they have a performance review at work and, if so, whether it is oral or written. Encourage them to discuss how they feel about getting a review. For example, ask if it makes them feel nervous, good, angry, etc.

Reading Practice (page 130)

Review with students if they get an oral or written review. Ask *Do you always understand the review? Who gives it to you?* If students get a written review, ask if it is anything like the form in the text.

Writing Practice (page 131)

Have students use the vocabulary and phrases from the exercise in reinforcement activities. As a class or in pairs, have them create one or more dialogues between a boss and and an employee. The employee can tell the boss his or her strengths. The boss will tell the employee about things he or she needs to improve. Students can role-play the dialogues in pairs and then reverse roles.

Bring in a written review or review form. Read it and discuss with the class. Ask how it is similar to or different from reviews used where they work.

Let's Think about It (page 132)

For extension, have students talk about things that are hard about living in the U.S. Encourage students who have experienced similar difficulties to suggest ways of dealing with problems.

Ask students if they know what to say or do for weddings, births, deaths, birthdays, and so on in this country. Have students share information. List appropriate ways to respond to those events. Have students practice them and create role-plays for different situations.

Have students compare and contrast acceptable workplace behavior in their native countries to that in the U.S. You may want to list or create charts to show some of the similarities and differences.

Application (page 133)

Students should be encouraged to write about any aspects of their own immigrant experience: coming to the U.S., what they like or don't like about life here, their jobs, their families, learning English, their ESL class, etc. Focus here on getting students to express their ideas without worrying about whether their English is perfect. If they wish, they can work with you later to edit the story and correct grammar and spelling.

For extension, help students compile their stories into a class book with a picture of each person before each story. This can provide ongoing reading material, models for further writing, and something to share with their families.

At Work in the U.S.
Unit Tests

The following unit tests may be photocopied for classroom activities and homework.

UNIT TEST

Vocabulary

Match each word with the correct definition.

_____ **1.** cafeteria   **a.** a paper for filling out information

_____ **2.** co-worker   **b.** boss

_____ **3.** department   **c.** things you need to do a job

_____ **4.** laundry   **d.** written name

_____ **5.** supervisor   **e.** a helper

_____ **6.** form   **f.** a person you work with

_____ **7.** uniform   **g.** a place to wash clothes

_____ **8.** aide   **h.** a place to eat at work

_____ **9.** signature   **i.** a part or division of a workplace

_____ **10.** supplies   **j.** clothes to wear at work

Measurements

Match the measurements that are the same.

_____ **1.** 1 ft.   **a.** 2 c.

_____ **2.** 1 tbsp.   **b.** 4 qt.

_____ **3.** 1 qt.   **c.** 144 sq. in.

_____ **4.** 1 pt.   **d.** 3 tsp.

_____ **5.** 1 yd.   **e.** 12 in.

_____ **6.** 1 sq. ft.   **f.** 2 pt.

_____ **7.** 1 gal.   **g.** 36 in.

Reading

Read the form and answer the questions.

NAME	Ho	Minh	
	Last	First	Middle Initial

ADDRESS	25	Water St.	30
	No.	Street	Apt. No.
	Palo Alto	CA	94303
	City	State	Zip Code

TEL. NO. __(415) 625-7300__   SOC. SEC. NO. __042-78-9545__
            Area Code

SEX   **MARITAL STATUS**

[X] Male   [ ] Married

[ ] Female   [X] Single

DATE OF BIRTH __6__ / __13__ / __65__   AGE __36__
                Mo.   Day   Yr.

NATIVE COUNTRY / COUNTRY OF BIRTH __Vietnam__

NAME OF EMPLOYER __Bancroft, Inc.__

SIGNATURE __Minh Ho__   DATE __10/8/01__

Answer the following questions.

1. What is Minh's last name? _____

2. Where does he live? _____

3. What is Minh's zip code? _____

4. What does *no.* mean? _____

5. Is Minh married or single? _____

6. How old is he? _____

7. Where does he work? _____

Writing

Answer the following questions. Write a complete sentence if you can.

1. What is your name?

   _____.

2. What country do you come from?

   _____.

3. What is your nationality?

   _____.

4. What is your address?

   _____.

5. Where do you work?

   _____.

Language Skills

Complete each sentence with the present tense form of the verb.

1. Luz _____ (be) my friend.

2. She _____ (be) thirty-two years old.

3. Luz and her husband, Miguel, _____ (live) in Miami.

4. Miami _____ (be) a big city.

5. Miguel _____ (work) in a hospital.

6. Luz _____ (want) to learn English and get a better job.

Make a question for each of the following sentences.

Example: You work every Saturday.   <u>Do</u> you <u>work</u> every Saturday?

1. Maria makes the fruit salad.

   _____ Maria _____ the fruit salad?

2. You like your job.

   _____ you _____ your job?

3. Your supervisor works hard.

   _____ your supervisor _____ hard?

4. They have three children.

   _____ they _____ three children?

UNIT TEST

Vocabulary

Match each word with the correct definition.

_____ **1.** storage room   **a.** Social Security

_____ **2.** benefit   **b.** time off with no pay

_____ **3.** deduct   **c.** supplies

_____ **4.** overtime   **d.** stop working for a short time

_____ **5.** FICA   **e.** less than 40 hours of work

_____ **6.** unpaid time   **f.** health insurance, vacation, etc.

_____ **7.** day off   **g.** place to keep supplies

_____ **8.** break   **h.** subtract; take away

_____ **9.** part-time   **i.** more than 40 hours of work

_____ **10.** materials   **j.** day with no work

Language Skills

Complete each sentence with the correct form of the verb _to have_.

Example: We <u>have</u> six paid holidays.

1. Rosa _____ the flu.

2. You _____ good benefits.

3. I _____ a lot of work to do today.

4. My manager _____ a day off today.

5. Sasha and Michael _____ the same vacations.

Complete each question with *can* + the verb.

Example: (leave) <u>Can</u> I <u>leave</u> at 3:30 tomorrow?

1. (cover for) _____ you _____ me on Thursday?

2. (go) _____ I _____ on break now?

3. (finish) _____ we _____ the order after lunch?

4. (take) _____ I _____ my vacation in July?

5. (help) _____ you _____ me?

Reading

Read the story and complete the pay stub.

Kwan Park gets paid every week. He makes $9.50 an hour and gets time and a half for overtime. From 11/7/02 to 11/13/02 Kwan worked 40 regular hours and 6 hours overtime. The deductions on his pay stub are Federal Withholding Tax for $28.06, State Tax for $15.35, FICA for $27.40 and Health Insurance for $68.75.

Employee Name	Kwan Park			**Deductions**	
Employee #				Fed. Withholding Tax	_____
Pay Period				FICA	_____

	Hours	**Rate**	**Total**
Regular	___ X ___		___
Overtime	___ X ___		___
GROSS PAY ➡			

State Withholding Tax _____

Health Insurance _____

Total Deductions _____

GROSS PAY ➡

TOTAL DEDUCTIONS ➡

NET PAY ➡

Writing

Answer the following questions. Write a complete sentence if you can.

1. What is the name of your department? _____

2. What is your job? _____

3. What supplies do you use at work?

_____

_____

4. What days do you work? _____

What hours do you work? _____

What are your days off? _____

5. You are late for work. What do you do?

_____

_____

You are sick and can't go to work. What do you do?

_____

_____

You want time off. What do you do?

_____

_____

UNIT TEST

Vocabulary

Match each word with the correct definition.

_____ **1.** toxic   **a.** right now

_____ **2.** caution   **b.** amount of heat or cold

_____ **3.** required   **c.** burns easily

_____ **4.** repair   **d.** warning; be careful

_____ **5.** fumes   **e.** poisonous

_____ **6.** immediately   **f.** fix

_____ **7.** temperature   **g.** harmful; dangerous

_____ **8.** flammable   **h.** necessary; need to do

_____ **9.** hazardous   **i.** something you breathe; gas and smoke

Complete each sentence with one of the words or phrases below.

rules	OSHA	training	first aid kit	fire extinguisher
labels	injuries	fire alarm	Quality Control	

1. You pull the _____ when there is a fire.

2. Following safety _____ helps to prevent accidents.

3. You need _____ to learn a new job.

4. People from _____ check for safety at a factory.

5. You use safety gear to prevent _____.

6. You keep medical supplies in a _____.

7. _____ have directions and safety warnings on them.

8. Use a _____ to put out a fire.

9. People from _____ check the products workers make.

Language Skills

Read the following paragraphs.

Karma *works* hard. She *makes* dresses. She *operates* a sewing machine. She *wears* a hairnet.

I *work* hard. I *make* furniture. I *use* a sanding machine. I *wear* a mask.

Kim and Helen *work* hard. They *clean* hotel rooms. They *use* mops and cleaners. They *wear* gloves.

Change each verb to the present continuous tense and rewrite the three paragraphs.

Karma is working hard. _____

_____

_____

_____

I _____

_____

_____

Kim and Helen _____

_____

_____

_____

Fill in the blanks with the past tense form of the verbs.

Vilma works in a restaurant. Yesterday she dropped a glass bowl. The bowl

(break) _____*broke*_____. Vilma (cut) _____ her hand. There

(is) _____ a lot of blood. A co-worker (put) _____

some cold water on Vilma's hand. Then she (tell) _____ the

manager about the accident. The manager (go) _____ to the

employee bathroom. He (get) _____ the first-aid kit and

(bring) _____ it to the kitchen. He (look) _____

for the bandages and (find) _____ a large one. He wrapped

Vilma's hand. Then he (take) _____ her to the hospital. At the

hospital Vilma and her manager (have) _____ to wait for an

hour. They (are) _____ both upset. Finally the doctor

(treat) _____ the cut on her hand. He (do) _____

a good job. After one week Vilma (go) _____ back to work.

After the accident Vilma (is) _____ more careful at work.

UNIT TEST

Vocabulary

Match each word with the correct definition.

_____ 1. evaluation   **a.** more pay

_____ 2. salary   **b.** helper

_____ 3. inventory   **c.** better job

_____ 4. damaged   **d.** do/get better

_____ 5. assistant   **e.** directions

_____ 6. raise   **f.** not good/broken

_____ 7. improve   **g.** list of items

_____ 8. promotion   **h.** review

_____ 9. instructions   **i.** wages

Choose the correct word to complete each sentence.

cooperative	hardworking	punctual
dependable	neat	

1. You work hard. You are _____.

2. You're always on time. You are _____.

3. Your work area is clean and in order. You are _____.

4. You work well with other people. You are _____.

5. You always come to work and do your job. You are _____.

Language Skills

What are you going to do in the future? Use the future tense.

Example: This afternoon I *am going to take* the bus home.

1. *Tonight* I _____.

2. *Tomorrow* I _____.

3. *Next weekend* I _____.

4. *Next summer* I _____.

5. *Next year* I _____.

Reading

Look at the bulletin board. Then answer the questions.

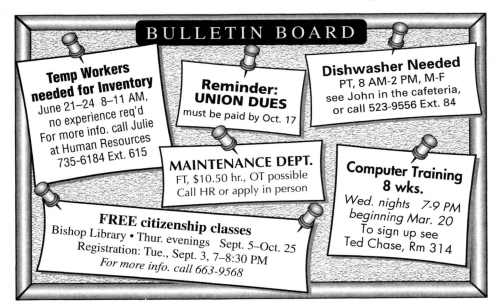

BULLETIN BOARD

Temp Workers needed for Inventory
June 21–24 8–11 AM,
no experience req'd
For more info. call Julie
at Human Resources
735-6184 Ext. 615

Reminder: UNION DUES
must be paid by Oct. 17

Dishwasher Needed
PT, 8 AM-2 PM, M-F
see John in the cafeteria,
or call 523-9556 Ext. 84

MAINTENANCE DEPT.
FT, $10.50 hr., OT possible
Call HR or apply in person

Computer Training 8 wks.
Wed. nights 7-9 PM
beginning Mar. 20
To sign up see
Ted Chase, Rm 314

FREE citizenship classes
Bishop Library • Thur. evenings Sept. 5–Oct. 25
Registration: Tue., Sept. 3, 7–8:30 PM
For more info. call 663-9568

1. How many weeks are the computer classes? What day are they on? Are they in the morning or at night?

2. Which job is full-time? Which jobs are part-time?

3. How much do the citizenship classes cost? Where are they? When do they take place? What number can you call for more information?

4. When must union dues be paid?

5. Which job is temporary and doesn't require experience?

Problem Solving

What do you do at work? Read the sentences below. Decide what to do. Check the best answer.

1. You can't find one of your supplies. What do you do?
   _____ a. Use something different.
   _____ b. Ask your boss.

2. Your boss gives directions. You don't understand everything. What do you do?
   _____ a. Ask a co-worker to explain them.
   _____ b. Ask the boss to explain them.

3. You have a problem with a co-worker. What do you do?
   _____ a. Talk to your boss.
   _____ b. Look for another job.

4. Your co-worker is smoking in a non-smoking area. You ask him to stop. He doesn't stop. What do you do?
   _____ a. Stop talking to your co-worker.
   _____ b. Tell your boss.

5. You are very late for work. Your boss will be mad. What do you do?
   _____ a. Take the day off.
   _____ b. Talk to your boss.

6. You are laid off. What do you do?
   _____ a. Go to the Unemployment office every week.
   _____ b. Call your old boss every week.

7. Your performance review is not good. What do you do?
   _____ a. Ask your boss how you can improve.
   _____ b. Look for another job.

At Work in the U.S.
Photocopy Masters

The following photocopy masters (PCMs) may be photocopied for classroom activities and homework.

UNIT 1 LESSON 1

Family Tree

Fill in the chart. Tell your classmates about your family.

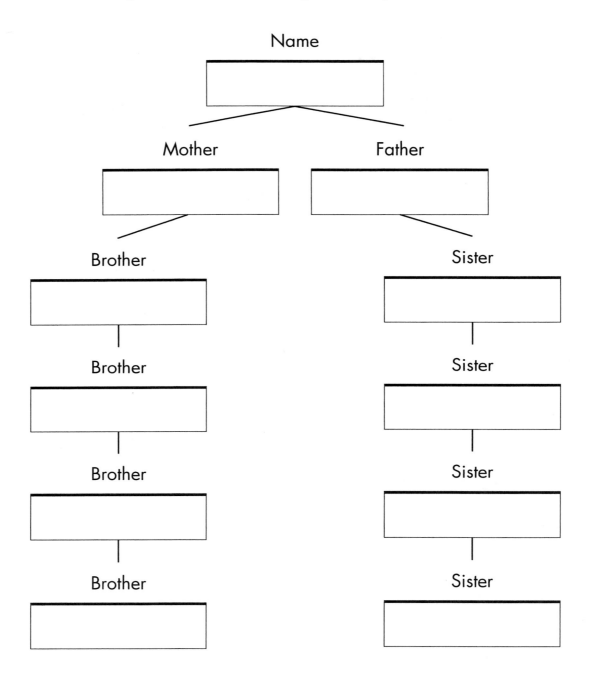

Name

Mother   Father

Brother   Sister

Brother   Sister

Brother   Sister

Brother   Sister

To the Teacher *Variation:* Copy the chart on the board. Students go to the board, fill in their information, and tell the class.

UNIT 1 LESSON 2

Vocabulary

Fill in the crossword puzzle with the correct words.

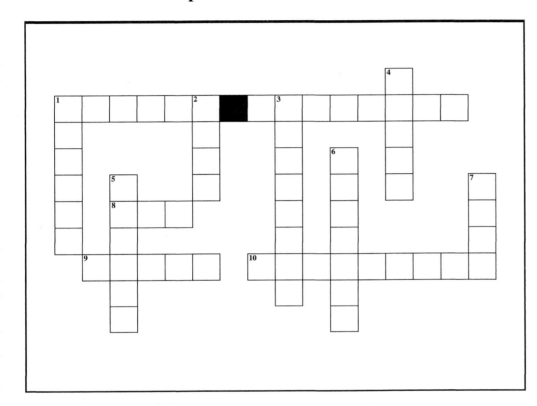

Across

age

birth

Social Security

telephone

Down

address

employer

family

first

last

male

single

Across

1. To work in the U.S., you need a _____ _____ number. (2 words)
8. How old are you? What is your _____?
9. Your birthday is your date of _____.
10. The area code is part of your _____ number.

Down

1. If you are not married, you are _____.
2. Garcia is Maria's _____ name.
3. The company where you work is your _____.
4. Maria is Maria Garcia's _____ name.
5. A father, mother, and children are a _____.
6. The place where you live is your _____.
7. Another word for man is _____.

UNIT 1 LESSON 3

Language Practice

Put the words in the correct order to make a sentence.

Example: kitchen Win the works in
<u>Win works in the kitchen.</u>

1. cafeteria co-workers in my the are

_____.

2. to talk supervisor wants Maria her to

_____.

3. supply room workers uniforms the in their get

_____.

4. a room there patient is new 35 in

_____.

5. punch in 7 A.M. workers and at punch out 3 P.M. at

_____.

6. co-workers class my of four ESL are my in

_____.

7. sheets hospital a and towels lot uses of the

_____.

To the Teacher *Variation:* Write each word on a card. (Index cards, poster board, or construction paper work well.) Students work in pairs and move cards around to make the sentence.

UNIT 1 LESSON 3

Vocabulary

Match the country with the corresponding nationality.

	Country		Nationality
____ 1.	Ukraine	**a.**	Japanese
____ 2.	Mexico	**b.**	Cambodian
____ 3.	Cambodia	**c.**	Sudanese
____ 4.	Brazil	**d.**	Korean
____ 5.	Japan	**e.**	Iranian
____ 6.	Guatemala	**f.**	Bosnian
____ 7.	Thailand	**g.**	Filipino
____ 8.	Iran	**h.**	Cape Verdean
____ 9.	Sudan	**i.**	Taiwanese
____ 10.	Pakistan	**j.**	Mexican
____ 11.	Korea	**k.**	Thai
____ 12.	Cape Verde	**l.**	Jordanian
____ 13.	Bosnia	**m.**	Peruvian
____ 14.	Taiwan	**n.**	Brazilian
____ 15.	The Philippines	**o.**	Turkish
____ 16.	Turkey	**p.**	Somali
____ 17.	Peru	**q.**	Ukrainian
____ 18.	Somalia	**r.**	Guatemalan
____ 19.	Jordan	**s.**	Pakistani

Do you know any people from these countries? Do you know where these countries are? Look at a map to find them.

UNIT 1 LESSON 4

Vocabulary

What kinds of food do you know? Work in teams. Write food words that begin with the following letters or pairs of letters. Write as many words as you can for each letter. The team with the most words wins. (*Variation:* If two or more teams have the same word, neither team gets the point.)

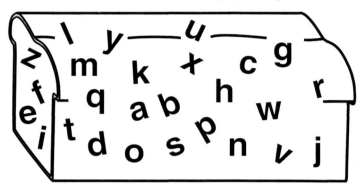

a _____   m _____

b _____   n _____

c _____   o _____

ch _____   p _____

d _____   r _____

e _____   s _____

f _____   sh _____

g _____   t _____

h _____   th _____

i _____   v _____

j _____   w _____

k _____   y _____

l _____   z _____

UNIT 1 LESSON 4

Measurements

A. Maria works in a kitchen. She needs to know measurements. Match each measurement to the correct abbreviation.

_____ 1. ounce   **a.** pt.

_____ 2. square   **b.** tbsp.

_____ 3. foot   **c.** yd.

_____ 4. teaspoon   **d.** lb.

_____ 5. tablespoon   **e.** doz.

_____ 6. gallon   **f.** qt.

_____ 7. pound   **g.** sq.

_____ 8. inch   **h.** tsp.

_____ 9. pint   **i.** c.

_____ 10. dozen   **j.** oz.

_____ 11. quart   **k.** in.

_____ 12. yard   **l.** gal.

_____ 13. cup   **m.** ft.

B. Match these measurements to the correct abbreviations.

_____ 1. centimeter   **a.** kg

_____ 2. Fahrenheit   **b.** m

_____ 3. liter   **c.** C

_____ 4. gram   **d.** F

_____ 5. meter   **e.** g

_____ 6. Celsius   **f.** L

_____ 7. kilogram   **g.** cm

What other measurements do you know?

UNIT 1 MORE PRACTICE

Vocabulary

Match each word with its opposite.

_____	**1.** last	**a.**	calm
_____	**2.** child	**b.**	punch out
_____	**3.** good	**c.**	difficult, hard
_____	**4.** female	**d.**	end
_____	**5.** fix	**e.**	first
_____	**6.** easy	**f.**	far
_____	**7.** inside	**g.**	adult
_____	**8.** sharp	**h.**	dirty
_____	**9.** old	**i.**	bad
_____	**10.** punch in	**j.**	single
_____	**11.** big	**k.**	outside
_____	**12.** different	**l.**	dull
_____	**13.** nervous	**m.**	early
_____	**14.** begin	**n.**	male
_____	**15.** near	**o.**	break
_____	**16.** clean	**p.**	new
_____	**17.** married	**q.**	same
_____	**18.** late	**r.**	small

On separate paper, write a sentence or pair of sentences using each word and its opposite.

UNIT 2 LESSON 5

Vocabulary

Circle the words that we use with the word *time*. Some words go across and some go down. Then write the words below.

s	h	o	d	a	y	l	p	g
o	v	e	r	n	f	u	l	l
m	b	h	d	i	n	n	e	r
e	r	f	j	s	i	c	d	b
c	e	l	n	i	g	h	t	a
v	a	c	a	t	i	o	n	p
f	k	a	l	r	e	n	s	a
t	w	f	s	i	c	k	e	r
b	o	k	f	u	p	a	n	t

break   over
day   part
dinner   sick
full   some
lunch   vacation
night

_____ day _____   _____   _____

_____   _____   _____

_____   _____   _____

_____   _____

Writing

Write the following dates in numbers.

Example: June 10, 2001   6/10/01

1. March 4, 1996   _____   **6.** December 7, 1941   _____

2. April 19, 2003   _____   **7.** September 26, 1970   _____

3. July 4, 1776   _____   **8.** January 31, 2010   _____

4. February 14, 2006   _____   **9.** November 4, 1978   _____

5. October 12, 1984   _____   **10.** August 14, 1964   _____

UNIT 2 LESSON 5

Work Schedule

Read the following work schedule. Then answer the questions.

WORK SCHEDULE					February 2-9	
	Mon.	**Tues.**	**Wed.**	**Thurs.**	**Fri.**	**Sat.**
Ana	7-3	7-3	7-3	9-5	off	7-3
Ming	9-5	off	9-5	7-3	9-5	9-5
Hana	12-8	12-8	12-8	12-8	7-3	off
Rose	7-3	7-3	off	7-3	12-8	7-3
Ken	12-8	9-5	12-8	12-8	off	12-8

1. Who works with Ming on Thursday? _____

2. Who works from 12—8 on Wednesday? _____

3. Who works from 7—3 on Saturday? _____

4. What day does Hana have off? _____

5. What hours does Ana work Monday through Wednesday? _____

6. What hours does Ming work for most of the week? _____

7. When does Ken start work on Tuesday? _____

8. When does Rose go home on Friday? _____

9. How many people work on Monday? _____

10. What days do Ken and Hana work the same shift? _____

To the Teacher *Extension:* Have students calculate how many hours a week each person works.

40 *At Work in the U.S.*

UNIT 2 LESSON 5

Personal Schedule

Do you have a busy schedule? Write down the things you do in one week. Include everything you do (shopping, laundry, cleaning, cooking, appointments, work, school, etc.).

Monday

Morning

Afternoon

Night

Tuesday

Morning

Afternoon

Night

Wednesday

Morning

Afternoon

Night

Thursday

Morning

Afternoon

Night

Friday

Morning

Afternoon

Night

Saturday

Sunday

UNIT 2 LESSON 6

Vocabulary

What supplies, equipment, and materials are there at work?
Work in teams. Write as many words as you can that begin with
each of the following letters. The team with the most words
wins. (*Variation:* If two or more teams have the same word,
neither team gets the point.)

a _____ m _____

b _____ n _____

c _____ o _____

ch _____ p _____

d _____ r _____

e _____ s _____

f _____ sh _____

g _____ t _____

h _____ th _____

i _____ v _____

j _____ w _____

k _____ y _____

l _____ z _____

UNIT 2 LESSON 7

Vocabulary

Put the letters in the correct order to make a vocabulary word.

Example: f i o c e f   <u>office</u>

1. k i s c   _____

2. y i d h o l a   _____

3. s m a g e s e   _____

4. n a c t i o v a   _____

5. n p o i t m e n p a t   _____

> **To the Teacher**   *Variation:* Write each letter on a card. (Index cards, poster board, or construction paper work well.) Students work in pairs and move cards around to make the word.

Writing Practice

Use this form to practice taking messages. Write the message your teacher or a partner dictates. Practice the kind of messages you take at work. (Suggested topics: calling in sick, requesting supplies, requesting service, etc.)

To _____ *(Your Boss's Name)*	Date _____
From _____ *(Your Name)*	Time _____ AM PM
Message _____ _____ _____ _____	

UNIT 2 LESSON 7

Interview

Make nine questions. Then interview a partner. Write your partner's answers next to each question.

How many	paid holidays personal days breaks paid sick days vacation days co-workers jobs supervisors years of experience	do you have?

1. _____ ? _____

2. _____ ? _____

3. _____ ? _____

4. _____ ? _____

5. _____ ? _____

6. _____ ? _____

7. _____ ? _____

8. _____ ? _____

9. _____ ? _____

To the Teacher *Extension:* Encourage follow-up questions and class discussion on these topics. (Examples: Are your breaks long enough? What do you do on vacation?)

Reading a Graph

This graph shows how Ana and Ramón spend their income each month. Look at the graph. Answer the questions.

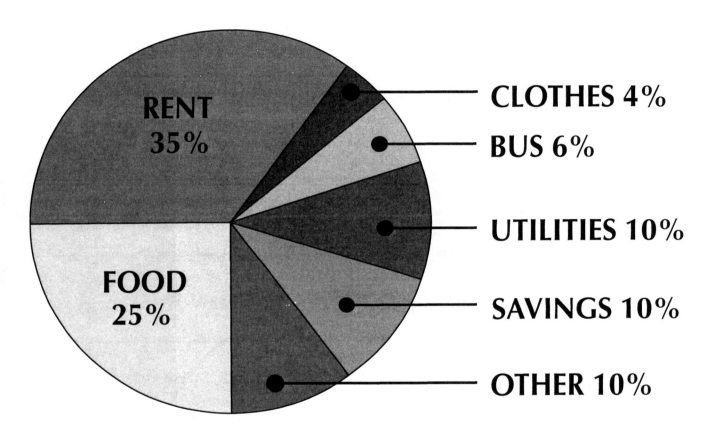

1. What percent (%) of their income do Ana and Ramón spend on food? On clothes?
2. Ana and Ramón take home $2,500 a month.
   a. How much money do they spend on rent?
   b. How much money do they spend on food?
   c. How much money do they spend on bus fare?
   d. How much money do they save?

UNIT 2 LESSON 8

Making a Budget

How do you spend your income each month? Fill in the chart below. Then make your own graph.

Expense	Amount (optional)	%
Rent		
Utilities (Phone, Electricity, Gas, etc.)		
Food		
Clothes		
Transportation		
Other		

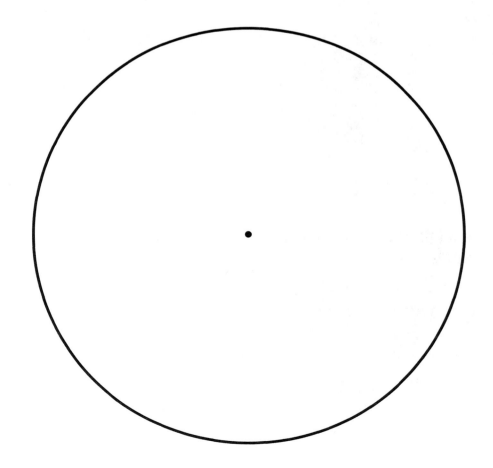

UNIT 2 LESSON 8

Math Problems

1. Sang earns $9.50 an hour. How much does he earn for 38 hours of work?

   Answer: _____

2. Vladimir paid $175 every month for 36 months to pay off a loan. What was the total amount he paid?

   Answer: _____

3. Sima's gross pay is $1,950 a month. Her deductions total $661. What is her net pay each month?

   Answer: _____

4. Last year Sam made $8.75 an hour. He worked 40 hours a week. He worked 50 weeks and had 2 weeks of paid vacation. What was Sam's gross pay for the year?

   Answer: _____

5. Bill makes $10.50 an hour and time and a half for overtime. He worked 40 regular hours and 8 hours of overtime last week. How much did he earn?

   Answer: _____

6. Reiko's net pay is $610.23. Her deductions are: $18.15 for state tax, $25.52 for federal tax, $43.10 for FICA, and $63.00 for medical insurance. What is Reiko's gross pay?

   Answer: _____

7. Gloria needs to buy a new coat. She has saved $50. The coat she wants costs $120. There is a 5% sales tax. How much more money does Gloria need to save before she can buy the coat?

   Answer: _____

UNIT 2 MORE PRACTICE

Language Practice

Put the words in the correct order to make a sentence.

Example: bad   have   I   a   stomachache   <u>I have a bad stomachache.</u>

1. take   now   can   break   I   my

   _____?

2. Saturday   you   me   can   for   on   cover

   _____?

3. have   this   I   to   at   leave   3:30   afternoon

   _____.

4. third   today   he   floor   working   the   is   on

   _____.

5. 9:00   doctor's   morning   have   at   a   tomorrow   I   appointment

   _____.

6. because   flu   work   I   the   come   have   can't   to   I

   _____.

7. the   paper towels   on   in   third   are   the   shelf   storage room   the

   _____.

To the Teacher   *Variation:* Write each word on a card. (Index cards, poster board, or construction paper work well.) Students work in pairs and move cards around to make the sentence.

UNIT 2 MORE PRACTICE

Vocabulary

Match each word with its opposite.

_____	**1.** add	**a.** healthy
_____	**2.** clean	**b.** more
_____	**3.** less	**c.** smaller
_____	**4.** early	**d.** bottom
_____	**5.** expensive	**e.** subtract, deduct
_____	**6.** full-time	**f.** dry
_____	**7.** day	**g.** correct, right
_____	**8.** paid	**h.** night
_____	**9.** sick	**i.** in front of
_____	**10.** save	**j.** part-time
_____	**11.** up	**k.** after
_____	**12.** wet	**l.** below
_____	**13.** above	**m.** spend
_____	**14.** bigger	**n.** unpaid
_____	**15.** before	**o.** late
_____	**16.** top	**p.** dirty
_____	**17.** behind	**q.** down
_____	**18.** wrong	**r.** cheap

On separate paper, write a sentence or pair of sentences using each word and its opposite.

UNIT 2 MORE PRACTICE

Vocabulary

Write the correct vocabulary word on the line next to each sentence. Write the circled letters on the lines at the bottom. What word does this make?

holiday	personal	sick	breaks
medicine	health	off	vacation

1. Some workers have two _____ each day. (b) _ _ _ _ _

2. _____ insurance helps pay for medicine and doctor bills. _ O _ _ _ _

3. You can take a _____ day to go to the dentist. _ _ _ _ _ O _ _

4. Sometimes the doctor gives you _____. _ O _ _ _ _ _ _

5. A day you don't work is a day _____. _ O _

6. Thanksgiving is a paid _____. _ _ _ O _ _ _

7. You want to visit your native country. You take _____ time. _ _ _ _ O _ _ _

8. You have the flu and stay home. You take a _____ day. O _ _ _

b _ _ _ _ _ _ _ _

To the Teacher *Extension:* Encourage follow-up questions and discussion of students' benefits; e.g., When are your breaks? How do you ask for a day off?

UNIT 3 LESSON 9

Reading Signs

Match each sign with its meanings.

1. _____ | CAUTION: Slippery Floor |

2. _____ | Harmful if swallowed |

3. _____ | NO ADMITTANCE |

4. _____ | Ear Protection Required |

5. _____ | *HIGH VOLTAGE* |

6. _____ | DANGER : Combustible |

7. _____ | **Do not operate this machinery without eye protection.** |

8. _____ | WATCH YOUR STEP |

9. _____ | CAUTION: *Hot Surface* |

10. _____ | No Food or Drink! |

a. You must not eat or drink in this area.

b. Be careful. This is very hot. You can burn yourself.

c. The floor is wet. Be careful.

d. You must use your safety glasses.

e. Be careful walking.

f. Do not eat or drink this product.

g. There is a lot of electrical power here.

h. Do not come in; do not enter.

i. You must wear earplugs or earmuffs.

j. This material can burn easily; it is flammable.

UNIT 3 LESSON 9

Vocabulary

A. Put the letters in the correct order to make a vocabulary word.
Example: g c h n a e   <u>change</u>

1. l e l a b   _____

2. a m a l r   _____

3. n a r w i n g   _____

4. y a s t e f   _____

5. o t c a u i n   _____

6. m b f a l e m a l   _____

7. a r o z d a s h u   _____

> **To the Teacher** *Variation:* Write each letter on a card. (Index cards, poster board or construction paper work well.) Students work in pairs and move cards around to make the word.

B. One word in each sentence is wrong. Cross it out and write the correct word above it. Use vocabulary from Lesson 9.

Example: Employees make products in a ~~hotel.~~ **factory**

1. Something that burns easily is different.

2. A change is a group of people working together.

3. Many labels have safety benefits on them.

4. You use a fire alarm to put out a fire.

5. Drinking or eating food makes you sick.

UNIT 3 LESSON 10

What's Wrong with this Picture?

**Look at the picture. There are eight safety hazards. Work with
your class to find them. Write them on the lines below.**

1. _____

2. _____

3. _____

4. _____

5. _____

6. _____

7. _____

8. _____

To the Teacher *Extension:* Discuss various solutions to the problems in the
picture. Using the picture, help the class make a list of safety rules. Add
others from your students' workplace(s).

At Work in the U.S. **53**

UNIT 3 LESSON 11

Vocabulary

Complete the sentences with the correct safety gear.

1. Carla works near noisy machines. She wears _____.

2. Metal can get in Oscar's eyes. He has to wear _____ for protection.

3. Tina often lifts patients in the nursing home. She wears a

    _____ to protect her back.

4. Tam works in a warehouse. He has to wear _____ to protect his feet.

5. Trina mixes chemicals. She has to wear _____ on her hands.

6. Alex works in construction. He always wears a _____ because things can fall on his head.

7. Bella works on an assembly line. She wears a _____ so her hair doesn't get caught in the machine.

8. Roberto paints cars. Paint fumes are toxic. Roberto wears a

    _____ so he won't breathe the fumes.

9. Miguel makes wooden furniture. There is a lot of dust. He wears a

    _____.

    What safety gear do you wear? Why?

UNIT 3 LESSON 11

Reading

Read the following insurance claim form. Answer the questions.

Claim Form

1. Name <u>Shur</u>   <u>Max</u>   <u>V</u>   Soc. Sec. No. <u>049-78-3562</u>
   Last   *First*   *MI*

2. Address <u>25</u> <u>Fort Pond Rd.</u> <u>Apt. 35</u> <u>Chicago</u>   <u>IL</u>   <u>60603</u>
   No.   *Street*   *City*   *State*   *Zip*

3. Tel. No <u>(773) 354-9302</u>   4. Date of Birth <u>6/21/68</u>

5. Health Insurance <u>HealthCare, Inc. 200 Main St. Chicago IL 60607</u>
   Company   *No. Street*   *City*   *State*   *Zip*

6. Member No <u>7403356698</u>

7. Physician <u>Dr. Philip Davis</u>   <u>2 Cox St.</u>   <u>Chicago</u>   <u>IL</u>   <u>60601</u>
   Name   *No. Street*   *City*   *State*   *Zip*

8. Employer <u>Chase Plastics Co. 78 West St. Chicago</u>   <u>IL</u>   <u>60607</u>
   Name   *No. Street*   *City*   *State*   *Zip*

9. Date of Injury <u>10/25/03</u>

10. Description of Injury <u>Back strain</u>

11. Temporary Disability (yes) no   Starting Date <u>10/26/03</u>

12. Permanent Disability   yes (no)   Starting Date _____

13. Physician's Signature <u>*Philip Davis*</u>

14. Applicant's Signature <u>*Max V. Shur*</u>

---

1. Who was hurt? _____

2. What is the injury? _____

3. When was the injury? _____

4. Who is the employer? _____

5. Is the disability temporary or permanent? _____

UNIT 3 LESSON 12

Reading

Look at the form below. Answer the questions.

SERVICE REQUEST

Name _Lin Wang_____

Date _8/24/01_____   Time _11:36 AM_____

Location of Problem _West Wing — Room 345_____

Description of Problem ___There is a spill on the floor._____

_____   _It looks like blood._____

---

1. What is the problem? _____

2. Where did it happen? _____

3. When did it happen? _____

4. Who reported the problem? _____

Writing

Think of a problem at work that requires service.
Complete the form below.

SERVICE REQUEST

Name _____

Date _____   Time _____

Location of Problem _____

Description of Problem _____

_____

UNIT 3 MORE PRACTICE

Vocabulary

Circle the word that does not belong.

Example: machine operator   (temperature)   team leader   supervisor

1. harmful   healthy   dangerous   hazardous

2. boots   glasses   goggles   mask

3. supplies   equipment   materials   mistakes

4. machine   plastic   metal   paper

5. hammer   screwdriver   pliers   safety

Vocabulary

Circle the safety gear and protective clothing. Then write the words on the lines below.

shirt	apron	backbrace	sneakers	shorts	gloves
earplugs	jeans	sweatshirt	skirt	boots	pants
mask	socks	safety glasses	hairnet	respirator	sweater
hard hat	t-shirt	safety goggles	raincoat	pajamas	earmuffs

_____   _____

_____   _____

_____   _____

_____   _____

_____   _____

_____   _____

UNIT 3 MORE PRACTICE

Vocabulary

Match each word with its opposite.

_____ 1. open   **a.** fail

_____ 2. careful   **b.** solution

_____ 3. put on   **c.** take out

_____ 4. exit   **d.** shut, close

_____ 5. harmful   **e.** start

_____ 6. comfortable   **f.** turn down

_____ 7. lost   **g.** unimportant

_____ 8. pass   **h.** entrance, enter

_____ 9. plug in   **i.** turn off

_____ 10. stop   **j.** careless

_____ 11. turn on   **k.** easy

_____ 12. turn up   **l.** uncomfortable

_____ 13. put in   **m.** take off

_____ 14. noisy   **n.** safe

_____ 15. problem   **o.** quiet

_____ 16. important   **p.** found

_____ 17. hard   **q.** unplug

On separate paper, write a sentence or pair of sentences using each word and its opposite.

UNIT 3 MORE PRACTICE

Vocabulary

Fill in the crossword puzzle with the correct words.

Across

earplugs

glasses

mask

respirator

rules

toxic

Down

accident

alarm

factory

mistake

prevent

repair

Across

  2. It is important to follow safety _____ at work.

  5. You wear _____ to protect your ears.

  7. Something that is poisonous is _____.

  9. A _____ helps you breathe.

 11. You wear safety _____ to protect your eyes.

 12. A _____ covers your mouth and nose.

Down

  1. Safety gear and equipment help to _____ accidents.

  3. To fix something is to _____ it.

  4. A _____ is a building where things are made.

  6. Safety gear protects you in case there is an _____.

  8. To do something wrong is to make a _____.

 10. When there is a fire, pull the fire _____.

UNIT 3 MORE PRACTICE

Math Problems

1. This chart shows the number of machine breakdowns at Jamestown, Inc. last year.

Jan. 1	Apr. 0	July 0	Oct. 2
Feb. 3	May 2	Aug. 1	Nov. 0
Mar. 2	June 4	Sept. 3	Dec. 1

What is the total number of breakdowns for the year?

Answer: _____

2. Al put three molds in the press at 10:10 A.M. He set the stop time for 11:40 A.M. How long were the molds in the press?

Answer: _____

3. Crowley Construction Company ordered five boxes of goggles. There are 24 pairs of goggles in each box. How many pairs of goggles did the company order?

Answer: _____

4. Rico has a board that is 62.25 inches long. He cuts off 25.75 inches. How many inches are left? How many feet?

Answer: _____

5. Clara's machine stopped working at 2:10. The machine was fixed, and Clara began working again at 3:45. How much production time did Clara lose?

Answer: _____

6. Last week Freeport Manufacturing Company made 6,500 fire extinguishers. This week they made 15% more. How many fire extinguishers did they make this week?

Answer: _____

UNIT 3 MORE PRACTICE

Test Yourself on Safety

Do you know about safety where you work?
Answer the following questions.

	Yes	No	Sometimes
1. Do you know the safety rules at work?			
2. Do you follow the safety rules at work?			
3. Do you know where the nearest exit is?			
4. Do you know where the nearest fire extinguisher is?			
5. Do you know where the first aid kit is?			
6. Do you have safety gear or protective clothing?			
7. Do you wear it?			
8. Is the place where you work			
a. quiet?			
b. clean and neat?			
9. Where you work, do you have			
a. good air?			
b. good lighting?			
10. Do you report safety problems?			

Did you answer *No* or *Sometimes* to any questions? If so,
what can you do to change your answer to *Yes*? Discuss
with your class.

To the Teacher *Extension:* Encourage students to explain why they answered
the way that they did. Ask them to describe the workplace conditions behind
their answers.

UNIT 4 LESSON 13

Writing

Fill out the form below with your personal information.

APPLICATION FOR EMPLOYMENT
PERSONAL INFORMATION

Name _____
Last   First   Middle Initial

Address _____
Street   Apt. #   City   State   Zip Code

Telephone _____ Social Security No. _____

Job Applied for _____ When can you start? _____

Days and Hours Available _____

WORK RECORD

Job_____   Job_____

Company _____   Company _____

Address _____   Address _____

Telephone _____   Telephone _____

Years _____   Years _____

REFERENCES

Name_____   Name _____

Address_____   Address_____

Telephone No. _____   Telephone No. _____

Relationship _____   Relationship _____

Signature _____   Date _____

UNIT 4 LESSON 14

Language Practice

Put the words in the correct order to make a complete sentence.

Example: shipment brought the Manny stockroom the to
<u>Manny brought the shipment to the stockroom.</u>

1. across   the   Women's Department   cafeteria   from   the   is

_____.

2. heavy   a   moved   furniture   the   dolly   Michael   with

_____.

3. front   the   in   store   Pharmacy   the   is   of   the

_____.

4. truck   Ahmad   tools   the   unloaded   from   of   boxes   the

_____.

5. restocked   the   yesterday   shelves   items   the   Yuri   and   checked

_____.

6. furniture   other   sells   tools   many   the   clothes   items   and   store

_____.

7. Magda   union   last   paid   and   joined   dues   the   week   her

_____.

To the Teacher *Variation:* Write each word on a card. (Index cards, poster board, or construction paper work well.) Students work in pairs and move cards around to make the sentence.

UNIT 4 LESSON 14

Vocabulary

What can you buy in a store? Work in teams. Write as many things as you can that begin with each of the following letters or pairs of letters. The team with the most words wins.

(*Variation:* If two teams have the same word, neither team gets a point.)

a _____   m _____

b _____   n _____

c _____   o _____

ch _____   p _____

d _____   r _____

e _____   s _____

f _____   sh _____

g _____   t _____

h _____   th _____

i _____   v _____

j _____   w _____

k _____   y _____

l _____   z _____

To the Teacher   *Extension:* Give students alternative settings for this exercise; e.g., a supermarket, a drug store, a department store, a building supply store.

UNIT 4 LESSON 15

Reading and Writing

Sometimes people write to newspapers. They write about things that are important to them. Read the following letter.

> *Dear City Times,*
> *I have a new friend at work. She is a very nice person. My friend is from another country. Her English isn't very good. Some people laugh at her when she tries to speak. This makes me mad.*
>
> *It isn't easy to learn another language. I came to this country 15 years ago. I know how hard it is to learn English. Everyone should help people learn a language, not laugh at them.*
> Julia

- **Why is Julia mad?**
- **Think of something that makes you mad. Talk about it with your classmates. Then write a letter.**

_____
(date)

Dear _____,
(newspaper)

_____

_____

_____

_____
(your name)

UNIT 4 LESSON 15

Cultural Exchange

1. Is work in the U.S. the same as work in your country? What is the same? What is different? Discuss with your classmates.

2. Is it OK to do the following things at your job in the U.S.? Was it OK to do them in your native country? Circle *yes* or *no*. Add ideas of your own. Discuss your answers with your classmates.

	At your job in the U. S.		At your job in your native country	
1. Shake hands when you meet someone	yes	no	yes	no
2. Come to work 10 minutes late	yes	no	yes	no
3. Ask for a raise	yes	no	yes	no
4. Ask a co-worker how much money he earns	yes	no	yes	no
5. Take unpaid vacation when you want to	yes	no	yes	no
6. Ask your boss for help	yes	no	yes	no
7. Take a break when you want to	yes	no	yes	no
8. Talk to your co-workers	yes	no	yes	no
9. Eat while working	yes	no	yes	no
10. Make a personal phone call	yes	no	yes	no
11. Call your supervisor if you're sick	yes	no	yes	no
12. Smoke at work	yes	no	yes	no
13. _____	yes	no	yes	no
14. _____	yes	no	yes	no
15. _____	yes	no	yes	no

UNIT 4 LESSON 16

Self-Evaluation

In this book you have learned about working in the U.S. Answer the questions below. Do you understand more about your job now? Can you do more now?

STUDENT SELF-EVALUATION

	Always	Sometimes	Never
1. I can fill out information on forms.			
2. I can give personal information clearly.			
3. I can talk about my job.			
4. I can ask questions about my paycheck.			
5. I can report an emergency.			
6. I can give directions.			
7. I am on time for work.			
8. I talk to my co-workers.			
9. I get along with people at work.			
10. I ask for time off.			
11. I call in sick.			
12. I take messages.			
13. I ask for help when I need it.			
14. I report problems.			
15. I follow safety rules.			
16. I wear protective clothing.			
17. I understand my schedule.			
18. I understand my benefits.			
19. I understand my pay stub.			
20. I understand labels and signs.			
21. I understand directions at work.			
22. I understand my review.			

UNIT 4 MORE PRACTICE

Vocabulary

Match each word with its opposite.

_____ **1.** available   **a.** light

_____ **2.** depressed   **b.** poor

_____ **3.** far   **c.** unload

_____ **4.** future   **d.** temporary

_____ **5.** hardworking   **e.** unavailable

_____ **6.** heavy   **f.** unpack

_____ **7.** in front of   **g.** past

_____ **8.** right   **h.** pull

_____ **9.** load   **i.** a lot

_____ **10.** neat   **j.** lazy

_____ **11.** skilled   **k.** receive

_____ **12.** permanent   **l.** lower, decrease

_____ **13.** punctual   **m.** happy

_____ **14.** push   **n.** near

_____ **15.** a few   **o.** short

_____ **16.** raise, increase   **p.** unskilled

_____ **17.** excellent   **q.** behind

_____ **18.** deliver   **r.** wrong

_____ **19.** pack   **s.** late

_____ **20.** long   **t.** messy

On separate paper, write a sentence or pair of sentences using each word and its opposite.

UNIT 4 MORE PRACTICE

Problems

Do the math. Then discuss the questions.

1. Nina works at the Big Bargain Department Store. Nina makes $425 a week. Her deductions and expenses total $410. There is a union at the store. The dues are $8.50 a week. If Nina joins the union, how much money will she have left?

   Answer: _____

   Do you think Nina should join the union? Why or why not?

2. Hector works in Shipping and Receiving. Each day he has orders to ship. Hector can put a total of 500 lbs. of merchandise on the truck. Today he has to ship these things:

   3 boxes of garden supplies @ 40 lbs. each   4 boxes of paint @ 40 lbs. each
   2 boxes of sports equipment @ 75 lbs. each   3 cases of oil @ 25 lbs. each
   4 boxes of work gloves @ 6½ lbs. each

   What is the total weight of the merchandise?

   Answer: _____

   Should Hector ship all the items? Why or why not?
   What would you do?

3. Blanca works in the stockroom. She makes $9.50 an hour and gets time and a half for overtime. Blanca usually works 48 hours a week. She can't make any more money in this job, so she wants to get a different job. There is an opening in Customer Service. The salary is $480 a week. Which pays more, the job in the stockroom or the job in Customer Service?

   Answer: _____

   In the new job Blanca can get a raise in three months. She can get promoted in a year. Do you think Blanca should take the new job? Why or why not?

MORE PRACTICE

Vocabulary

A compound word is a large word made up of two or more words.
Find the two words in each of the compound words below.

Example: workplace   <u>work</u> <u>place</u>

1. birthday	**16.** afternoon
2. hardworking	**17.** teamwork
3. backache	**18.** overtime
4. careless	**19.** breakdown
5. hairnet	**20.** headache
6. restroom	**21.** earplugs
7. layoff	**22.** paycheck
8. classroom	**23.** stomachache
9. forklift	**24.** housekeeper
10. babysit	**25.** weekend
11. tablecloth	**26.** screwdriver
12. stockroom	**27.** dishwasher
13. handsaw	**28.** bathroom
14. earache	**29.** keyboard
15. cookbook	**30.** pillowcase

Do you know other compound words?

To the Teacher   *Variation:* Many of the words here can be grouped by category (e.g., equipment, rooms, health problems). Have students categorize as many words as possible and then add words to those categories.

PCM 40
MORE PRACTICE

Writing

How would you make things better at work? Put your ideas
in the suggestion box.

SUGGESTION BOX

Department _____   Date_____

_____

_____

How will your suggestion help at work? Fill out the form
below. Check how your suggestion will make things better.

Making Things Better

_____ will save:
(My suggestion)

1. time   _____

2. energy (fuel, electricity, etc.)   _____

3. material   _____

4. paperwork   _____

5. waste   _____

6. mistakes   _____

_____ will also make things:
(My suggestion)

1. safer   _____

2. cleaner   _____

3. cheaper   _____

4. easier   _____

5. faster   _____

To the Teacher Encourage students to explain their answers.

MORE PRACTICE

Achievements

What have you done this year? Fill in the form below.

MY ACHIEVEMENTS

Work	Date	Description
1. New Skill	_____	_____
2. More Responsibility	_____	_____
3. New Job	_____	_____
4. Raise	_____	_____
5. Promotion	_____	_____
6. Other	_____	_____

Personal Life	Date	Description
1. Driver's License	_____	_____
2. Citizenship	_____	_____
3. New Car	_____	_____
4. New House	_____	_____
5. Other	_____	_____

Participation in	Description
1. ESL Class	_____
2. Other education / Training	_____
3. Child's education / School	_____
4. New social activity in the U.S.	_____
5. Other	_____

To the Teacher *Extension:* Have students make a list of future goals.

Answer Key For Unit Tests

UNIT 1 TEST

Vocabulary
1. h
2. f
3. i
4. g
5. b
6. a
7. j
8. e
9. d
10. c

Measurements
1. e
2. d
3. f
4. a
5. g
6. c
7. b

Reading
1. Ho
2. 25 Water St., Apt. 30, Palo Alto, CA, 94303
3. 94303
4. number
5. single
6. 36
7. Bancroft, Inc.

Writing
Answers will vary.

Language Skills
1. is
2. is
3. live
4. is
5. works
6. wants

1. Does / make
2. Do / like
3. Does / work
4. Do / have

UNIT 2 TEST

Vocabulary
1. g
2. f
3. h
4. i
5. a
6. b
7. j
8. d
9. e
10. c

Language Skills
1. has
2. have
3. have
4. has
5. have

1. Can / cover for
2. Can / go
3. Can / finish
4. Can / take
5. Can / help

Reading
11/7/02 – 11/13/02
40, $9.50, $380
6, $14.25, $85.50
$465.50
$28.06
$27.40
$15.35
$68.75
$139.56
$465.50, $139.56, $325.94

Writing Skills
Answers will vary

UNIT 3 TEST

Vocabulary
1. e
2. d

3. h

4. f

5. i

6. a

7. b

8. c

9. g

1. fire alarm

2. rules

3. training

4. OSHA

5. injuries

6. first aid kit

7. Labels

8. fire extinguisher

9. Quality Control

Language Skills

is making

is operating

is wearing

am working

am making

am using

am wearing

are working

are cleaning

are using

are wearing

cut

was

put

told

went

got

brought

looked

found

took

had

were

treated

did

went

was

UNIT 4 TEST

Vocabulary

1. h

2. i

3. g

4. f

5. b

6. a

7. d

8. c

9. e

1. hardworking

2. punctual

3. neat

4. cooperative

5. dependable

Language Skills

Answers will vary; use future tense.

Reading

1. 8 weeks Wednesday nights

2. full-time – maintenance
part-time – dishwasher, inventory

3. free, Bishop Library, Thursday evenings,
9/5 – 10/25, 663-9568

4. by 10/17

5. inventory

Problem Solving

1. b

2. b

3. a

4. b

5. b

6. a

7. a

Answer Key For PCMs

UNIT 1 LESSON 2 (PCM 2)

Vocabulary

```
                              F
  S O C I A L ▇ S E C U R I T Y
  I       A     M         R
  N       S     P A       S
  G   F   T     L D       T   M
  L A G E       O D           A
  E M           Y R           L
    B I R T H   T E L E P H O N E
    L           R           S
    Y                       S
```

UNIT 1 LESSON 3 (PCM 3)

Language Practice

1. My co-workers are in the cafeteria.
2. Maria wants to talk to her supervisor.
3. Workers get their uniforms in the supply room.
4. There is a new patient in Room 35.
5. Workers punch in at 7 A.M. and punch out at 3 P.M.
6. Four of my co-workers are in my ESL class.
7. The hospital uses a lot of sheets and towels.

UNIT 1 LESSON 3 (PCM 4)

Vocabulary

1. q
2. j
3. b
4. n
5. a
6. r
7. k
8. e
9. c
10. s
11. d
12. h
13. f
14. i
15. g
16. o
17. m
18. p
19. l

UNIT 1 LESSON 4 (PCM 6)

Measurements

A.
1. j
2. g
3. m
4. h
5. b
6. l
7. d
8. k
9. a
10. e
11. f
12. c
13. i

B.
1. g
2. d
3. f
4. e
5. b
6. c
7. a

UNIT 1 MORE PRACTICE (PCM 7)

Vocabulary

1. e
2. g
3. i
4. n
5. o
6. c
7. k
8. l
9. p
10. b
11. r
12. q

13. a

14. d

15. f

16. h

17. j

18. m

UNIT 2 LESSON 5 (PCM 8)

Vocabulary

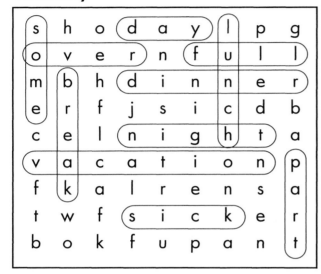

Writing

1. 3/4/96

2. 4/19/03

3. 7/4/76

4. 2/14/06

5. 10/12/84

6. 12/7/41

7. 9/26/70

8. 1/31/10

9. 11/4/78

10. 8/14/64

UNIT 2 LESSON 5 (PCM 9)

Work Schedule

1. Rose

2. Hana

3. Ana and Rose

4. Saturday

5. 7-3

6. 9-5

7. nine o'clock

8. eight o'clock

9. 5

10. Mon., Wed., Thurs.

UNIT 2 LESSON 7 (PCM 12)

Vocabulary

1. sick

2. holiday

3. message

4. vacation

5. appointment

UNIT 2 LESSON 7 (PCM 13)

Interview

1. How many paid holidays do you have?

2. How many personal days do you have?

3. How many breaks do you have?

4. How many paid sick days do you have?

5. How many vacation days do you have?

6. How many co-workers do you have?

7. How many jobs do you have?

8. How many supervisors do you have?

9. How many years of experience do you have?

UNIT 2 LESSON 8 (PCM 14)

Reading a Graph

1. 25%, 4%

2. a. $875

b. $625

c. $150

d. $250

UNIT 2 LESSON 8 (PCM 16)

Math Problems

1. $361

2. $6,300

3. $1,289

4. $18,200

5. $546

6. $760

7. $76

UNIT 2 MORE PRACTICE (PCM 17)

Language Practice

1. Can I take my break now?
2. Can you cover for me on Saturday?
3. I have to leave at 3:30 this afternoon. / This afternoon I have to leave at 3:30.
4. He is working on the third floor today. / Today he is working on the third floor.
5. I have a doctor's appointment at 9:00 tomorrow morning.
6. I can't come to work because I have the flu.
7. The paper towels are on the third shelf in the storage room.

UNIT 2 MORE PRACTICE (PCM 18)

Vocabulary

1. e
2. p
3. b
4. o
5. r
6. j
7. h
8. n
9. a
10. m
11. q
12. f
13. l
14. c
15. k
16. d
17. i
18. g

UNIT 2 MORE PRACTICE (PCM 19)

Vocabulary

1. breaks
2. health
3. personal
4. medicine
5. off
6. holiday
7. vacation
8. sick
benefits

UNIT 3 LESSON 9 (PCM 20)

Reading Signs

1. c
2. f
3. h
4. i
5. g
6. j
7. d
8. e
9. b
10. a

UNIT 3 LESSON 9 (PCM 21)

Vocabulary

A.
1. label
2. alarm
3. warning
4. safety
5. caution
6. flammable
7. hazardous

B.
1. Something that burns easily is <u>flammable.</u>
2. A <u>team</u> is a group of people working together.
3. Many labels have safety <u>warnings</u> on them.
4. You use a fire <u>extinguisher</u> to put out a fire.
5. Drinking or eating <u>poison</u> makes you sick.

UNIT 3 LESSON 10 (PCM 22)

What's Wrong with this Picture?

1. A man is smoking near a non-smoking sign.
2. Boxes are in front of the emergency exit.
3. A worker is climbing on the top step of a ladder and reaching too far.
4. A worker is drinking coffee in the work area.
5. Sharp tools and equipment are left out and plugged in on tables.
6. Chemicals are in uncovered containers.

7. There is a spill on the floor.

8. The fire extinguisher is missing.

UNIT 3 LESSON 11 (PCM 23)

Vocabulary

1. earmuffs or
earplugs

2. glasses or
goggles

3. back support belt

4. boots

5. gloves

6. hard hat

7. hairnet

8. respirator

9. mask

UNIT 3 LESSON 11 (PCM 24)

Claim Form

1. Max Shur

2. Back strain

3. 10/25/03

4. Chase Plastics Co.

5. temporary

UNIT 3 LESSON 12 (PCM 25)

Reading

1. There is a spill on the floor.

2. West Wing, Room 345

3. at 11:36 A.M. on 8/24/01 / August 24, 2001

4. Lin Wang

UNIT 3 MORE PRACTICE (PCM 26)

Vocabulary

1. healthy

2. boots

3. mistakes

4. machine

5. safety

Vocabulary

apron

backbrace

gloves

earplugs

boots

mask

safety glasses

hairnet

respirator

hard hat

safety goggles

earmuffs

UNIT 3 MORE PRACTICE (PCM 27)

Vocabulary

1. d

2. j

3. m

4. h

5. n

6. l

7. p

8. a

9. q

10. e

11. i

12. f

13. c

14. o

15. b

16. g

17. k

UNIT 3 MORE PRACTICE (PCM 28)

Vocabulary

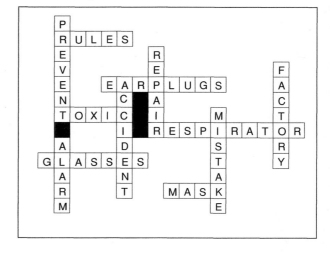

UNIT 3 MORE PRACTICE (PCM 29)

Math Problems
1. 19
2. 1 ¹/₂ hours / 1 hour and 30 minutes
3. 120 pairs
4. 36 ¹/₂ inches / 36.5 inches 3 feet ¹/₂ inch
5. 1 hour and 35 minutes
6. 7,475

UNIT 4 LESSON 14 (PCM 32)

Language Practice
1. The cafeteria is across from the Women's Department. / The Women's Department is across from the cafeteria.
2. Michael moved the heavy furniture with a dolly.
3. The Pharmacy is in the front of the store.
4. Ahmad unloaded the boxes of tools from the truck.
5. Yesterday Yuri checked the items and restocked the shelves.
6. The store sells tools, clothes, furniture, and many other items.
7. Last week Magda joined the union and paid her dues.

UNIT 4 LESSON 15 (PCM 34)

Reading
Julia is mad because people laugh at her friend when she speaks English.

UNIT 4 MORE PRACTICE (PCM 37)

Vocabulary
1. e
2. m
3. n
4. g
5. j
6. a
7. q
8. r
9. c
10. t
11. p
12. d
13. s
14. h
15. i
16. l
17. b
18. k
19. f
20. o

UNIT 4 MORE PRACTICE (PCM 38)

Problems
1. $6.50
2. 531 pounds (lbs.)
3. the job in the stockroom

MORE PRACTICE (PCM 39)

Vocabulary
1. birth   day
2. hard   working
3. back   ache
4. care   less
5. hair   net
6. rest   room
7. lay   off
8. class   room
9. fork   lift
10. baby   sit
11. table   cloth
12. stock   room
13. hand   saw
14. ear   ache
15. cook   book
16. after   noon
17. team   work
18. over   time
19. break   down
20. head   ache
21. ear   plugs
22. pay   check
23. stomach   ache
24. house   keeper
25. week   end
26. screw   driver
27. dish   washer
28. bath   room
29. key   board
30. pillow   case